COUNTRY

Formal Name: Republic of Yemen (Al Jumhuriyah al Yamaniyah).

Short Form: Yemen.

Term for Citizen(s): Yemeni(s).

Major Cities: The capital of Yemen is Sanaa. Other major cities are Aden, Taizz, Al Hudaydah, and Al Mukalla.

Independence: North Yemen gained independence from the Ottoman Empire in November 1918, and South Yemen became independent from Britain on November 30, 1967. The Republic of Yemen was established on May 22, 1990, with the merger of North Yemen (the Yemen Arab Republic) and South Yemen (the People's Democratic Republic of Yemen).

Public Holidays: Public holidays other than New Year's Day, International Women's Day, Labour Day, Corrective Movement Anniversary, and National Day are dependent on the Islamic calendar and vary from year to year. For 2008 the holidays are: New Year's Day (January 1); Muharram, Islamic New Year (January 10); Ashoura (January 19); International Women's Day (March 8); Mouloud, Birth of Muhammad (March 20); Labour Day (May 1); National Unification Day (May 22); Corrective Movement Anniversary (June 13); Leilat al Meiraj, Ascension of Muhammad (July 30); first day of Ramdan (September 1); Eid al Fitr, end of Ramadan (October 1); National Day (October 14); Eid al Adha, Feast of the Sacrifice (December 8); and Muharram, Islamic New Year (December 29).

Flag: Three equal horizontal bands of red (on top), white, and black.

Click to Enlarge Image

HISTORICAL BACKGROUND

Medieval History: In pre-Islamic times, the area that encompasses the present-day Republic of Yemen was called Arabia Felix—happy or prosperous Arabia—and was ruled by a number of indigenous dynasties in several different kingdoms. The most important cultural, social, and political event in Yemen's history was the coming of Islam around A.D. 630. Following the conversion of the Persian governor, many of the sheikhs and their tribes converted to Islam, and Yemen was ruled as part of Arab caliphates. The former North Yemen came under the control of imams of various dynasties, the most important of which were the Zaydis, whose dynasty lasted well into the twentieth century.

1

Former North Yemen: By the sixteenth century and again in the nineteenth century, northern Yemen was controlled in the cities by the Ottoman Empire and in tribal areas by the Zaydi imam's suzerainty. The Ottoman Empire was dissolved in 1918, and Imam Yahya, leader of the Zaydi community, took power in the area that later became the Yemen Arab Republic (YAR), or North Yemen. Underground opposition to Yahya began in the late 1930s, and by the mid-1940s major elements of the population opposed his rule. In 1948 Yahya was assassinated in a palace coup, and forces opposed to his feudal rule seized power. His son Ahmad succeeded him and ruled until his own death in September 1962. Imam Ahmad's reign was marked by growing repression, renewed friction with the British over their presence in the south, and increasing pressure to support the Arab nationalist objectives of Egyptian President Gamal Abdul Nasser. From 1958 to 1961, North Yemen was federated with Egypt and Syria in the United Arab States. Imam Ahmad's son Badr assumed power after Ahmad's death but was deposed one week later by army officers, led by Colonel Abdallah al Sallal, who took control of Sanaa and created the YAR. Immediately upon taking power, the officers created the ruling eight-member Revolutionary Command Council headed by Sallal. Civil war ensued between the royalist forces, supported by Saudi Arabia and Jordan in opposition to the newly formed republic, and republicans, supported by Egyptian troops. In 1967 Egyptian troops were withdrawn, and by 1968, following a royalist siege of Sanaa, most of the opposing leaders had reconciled. In 1970 Saudi Arabia recognized the YAR.

Former South Yemen: British influence increased in the southern and eastern portion of Yemen after the British captured the port of Aden in 1839. It was ruled as part of British India until 1937, when Aden became a crown colony, and the remaining territory was designated a protectorate (administered as the Eastern Protectorate and Western Protectorate). By 1965 most of the tribal states within the protectorate and the Aden colony itself had joined to form the British-sponsored Federation of South Arabia. Over the next two years, two rival factions—the Marxist National Liberation Front (NLF) and the Front for the Liberation of Occupied South Yemen (FLOSY)—fought for power. By August 1967, the NLF was in control of most areas, and at the end of the summer the federation formally collapsed. The last British troops were removed on November 29. On November 30, 1967, the People's Republic of Yemen, comprising Aden and South Arabia, was proclaimed. In June 1969, a radical wing of the NLF gained power. The country's name changed to the People's Democratic Republic of Yemen (PDRY) on December 1, 1970.

Road to Unification: By 1972 the two Yemens were in open conflict. The YAR received aid from Saudi Arabia, and the PDRY received arms from the Soviet Union. Although the Arab League brokered a cease-fire and both sides agreed to forge a united Yemen within 18 months, the two Yemens remained apart. The following years saw continued unrest and conflict, culminating in the assassination of the president of the YAR in June 1978. A month later, the Constituent People's Assembly elected Lieutenant Colonel Ali Abdallah Salih as president of the YAR. Renewed fighting broke out in early 1979, but in March the heads of state of the two Yemens signed an agreement in Kuwait pledging unification.

In April 1980, Abdul Fattah Ismail, who had been appointed head of state of the PDRY in December 1978, resigned and went into exile. He was replaced by Ali Nasir Muhammad, a former prime minister. In January 1986, Ismail returned from exile and resumed a senior position in the Yemen Socialist Party (YSP). More than a month of violence between Muhammad and Ismail's supporters resulted in Muhammad's ouster and Ismail's death. In February 1986, former prime minister Haydar Abu Bakr al Attas was named president of a newly formed PDRY government. In October a general election took place in the PDRY for the national legislature. In the YAR's first general election, held in July 1988, President Salih won a third five-year term.

In May 1988, the governments of the YAR and PDRY agreed to withdraw troops from their mutual border, create a demilitarized zone, and allow easier border crossings for citizens of both states. In May 1990, they agreed on a draft unity constitution, which was ultimately approved by referendum in May 1991. The Republic of Yemen was officially declared on May 22, 1990. President Salih of the YAR became president of the new republic; Ali Salim al Baydh, secretary general of the Central Committee of the YSP was named vice president; and PDRY President al Attas was named prime minister. Al Attas led a transitional coalition Council of Ministers whose membership was divided between the General People's Congress (GPC; the party supporting President Salih) and the YSP (the party supporting Vice President al Baydh).

Unrest and Civil War: In late 1991 through early 1992, deteriorating economic conditions led to significant domestic unrest, including several riots. Legislative elections were nonetheless held in early 1993, and in May the two former ruling parties, the GPC and the YSP, merged to create a single political party with an overall majority in the new House of Representatives. In August Vice President al Baydh exiled himself voluntarily to Aden, and the country's general security situation deteriorated as political rivals settled scores and tribal elements took advantage of the widespread unrest. In January 1994, representatives of the main political parties signed a document of pledge and accord in Amman, Jordan, that was designed to resolve the ongoing crisis. But by May 1994, the country was in civil war, and international efforts to broker a cease-fire were unsuccessful. On May 21, 1994, al Baydh and other leaders of the former South Yemen declared secession and the establishment of a new Democratic Republic of Yemen centered in Aden, but the new republic failed to achieve any international recognition. On July 7, 1994, President Salih's troops captured Aden, thus ending the civil war. In August 1994, in an attempt to undermine the strength of southern military units loyal to the YSP, President Salih prohibited party membership within the armed forces; he also introduced amendments to the constitution abolishing the Presidential Council and establishing universal suffrage. In October he was reelected president and named GPC members to key cabinet posts; several ministerial posts were given to members of the Yemeni Islah Party (YIP), which had been loyal to Salih during the civil war.

1994 to Present: Following the civil war, Yemen's currency, the riyal, was devalued; the cost of fuel doubled, water and electricity were in short supply, and food costs rose. Public demonstrations ensued, and the YIP was at odds with the GPC over economic reforms recommended by the World Bank. In the April 1997 parliamentary elections, the GPC garnered 187 seats and the YIP only 53 seats. A new Council of Ministers composed primarily of GPC members was named in May. The country continued to experience unrest due to economic hardship, coupled with increasing lawlessness, particularly against tourists. In September 1999, the first direct presidential election was held, reelecting the incumbent, President Salih, to a five-year term by an overwhelming margin. Constitutional amendments adopted in 2000 extended the president's term by two years. President Salih was reelected in September 2006. In October

2007, he announced comprehensive political reforms, some of which will not take effect until he is no longer in power, calling into question the prospects for implementation. The September 2006 elections for local and governorate council seats, as well as the May 2008 elections for governorate governors have left power largely in the hands of the ruling GPC.

GEOGRAPHY

Location: Yemen is located in the Middle East at the southern tip of the Arabian Peninsula between Oman and Saudi Arabia. It is situated at the entrance to the Bab el Mandeb strait, which links the Red Sea to the Indian Ocean (via the Gulf of Aden) and is one of the most active and strategic shipping lanes in the world.

Click to Enlarge Image

Size: Yemen has an area of 527,970 square kilometers, including the islands of Perim at the southern end of the Red Sea and Socotra at the entrance to the Gulf of Aden.

Land Boundaries: Yemen's land boundaries total 1,746 kilometers. Yemen borders Saudi Arabia to the north (1,458 kilometers) and Oman to the northeast (288 kilometers).

Disputed Territory: A long-standing dispute between Saudi Arabia and Yemen was resolved in June 2000 with the signing of the Treaty of Jiddah. This agreement provides coordinates for use in delineating the land and maritime border, including the section in the eastern desert region of Yemen that potentially contains significant amounts of oil. Friction between the two countries in recent years over security of the borders appears to have been alleviated by the establishment of joint border patrols. However, in early 2008 Saudi Arabia reinforced its concrete-filled security barrier along sections of the border in order to stem illegal cross-border activities.

Following years of dispute between Yemen and Eritrea over ownership of the Hanish Islands and fishing rights in the Red Sea, in 1999 an international arbitration panel awarded sovereignty of the islands to Yemen. In 2002 Yemen established an economic and security link with Sudan and Ethiopia; because all three countries have been involved in disputes with Eritrea, the alliance has caused renewed tensions in the region.

Length of Coastline: Yemen has 1,906 kilometers of coastline along the Arabian Sea, the Gulf of Aden, and the Red Sea.

Maritime Claims: Yemen claims a territorial sea of 12 nautical miles, a contiguous zone of 24 nautical miles, an exclusive economic zone of 200 nautical miles, and a continental shelf of 200 nautical miles or to the edge of the continental margin.

Topography: Yemen occupies the southern end of the Arabian Plateau. The country's mountainous interior is surrounded by narrow coastal plains to the west, south, and east and by upland desert to the north along the border with Saudi Arabia. The Tihamah is a nearly 419-kilometer-long, semidesert coastal plain that runs along the Red Sea. The interior mountains have elevations ranging from a few hundred meters to the country's highest point, Jabal an Nabi

4

Shuayb, which is 3,760 meters above sea level. The highland regions are interspersed with wadis, or river valleys, that are dry in the summer months. Most notable is the Wadi Hadhramaut in eastern Yemen, the upper portions of which contain alluvial soil and floodwaters and the lower portion of which is barren and largely uninhabited. Both the eastern plateau region and the desert in the north are hot and dry with little vegetation.

Principal Rivers: Yemen has no permanent rivers.

Climate: Temperatures are generally very high in Yemen, particularly in the coastal regions. Rainfall is limited, with variations based on elevation. The highlands enjoy a temperate, rainy summer with an average high temperature of 21° C and a cool, moderately dry winter with temperatures occasionally dipping below 4° C. The climate of the Tihamah (western coastal plain) is tropical; temperatures occasionally exceed 54° C, and the humidity ranges from 50 to 70 percent. Rainfall, which comes in irregular heavy torrents, averages 130 millimeters annually. In Aden the average temperature is 25° C in January and 32° C in June, but with highs often exceeding 37° C. Average annual rainfall is 127 millimeters. The highest mountainous areas of southern Yemen receive from 520 to 760 millimeters of rain a year. It is not uncommon for the northern and eastern sections of the country to receive no rain for five years or more. The Wadi Hadhramaut in the eastern part of Yemen is arid and hot, and the humidity ranges from 35 percent in June to 64 percent in January.

Natural Resources: Yemen's principal natural resources are oil and natural gas as well as agriculturally productive land in the west. Other natural resources include fish and seafood, rock salt, marble, and minor deposits of coal, gold, lead, nickel, and copper.

Land Use: Only 2.9 percent of Yemen is considered to be arable land, and less than 0.3 percent of the land is planted with permanent crops. About 5,500 square kilometers of land are irrigated. According to the United Nations, Yemen has 19,550 square kilometers of forest and other wooded land, which constitutes almost 4 percent of total land area.

Environmental Factors: Yemen is subject to sandstorms and dust storms, resulting in soil erosion and crop damage. The country has very limited natural freshwater and consequently inadequate supplies of potable water. Desertification (land degradation caused by aridity) and overgrazing are also problems.

Time Zone: Yemen is three hours ahead of Greenwich Mean Time.

SOCIETY

Population: Yemen's latest census, conducted in December 2004, reported a population of 19.72 million persons, reflecting an average annual population growth rate of more than 3 percent. The U.S. government has estimated a population of 22.2 million persons as of July 2007, and the International Monetary Fund estimated almost 21 million persons in 2005. Yemen's population has more than doubled since 1975 and has grown approximately 35 percent since the 1994 census, making Yemen the second most populous country on the Arabian

Peninsula. Adding to the growth of the native population is the influx of Somali refugees into Yemen—tens of thousands every year. According to the United Nations Refugee Agency, there were almost 96,000 African refugees in Yemen in 2006, including more than 91,000 Somalis. The Yemen government estimated 300,000 Somalis in Yemen in 2007. According to the United Nations, Yemen's population in 2005 was 27.3 percent urban and 73.7 percent rural; population density was 40 persons per square kilometer.

Demography: Yemen's population is predominantly young. According to U.S. government and United Nations estimates, in 2007 about 46 percent of the population was under age 15; slightly more than half the population, 15–64; and less than 3 percent, 65 and older. The population was almost equally divided between males and females. In 2007 the birthrate and death rate were estimated to be 42.7 per 1,000 and 8.1 per 1,000, respectively. The infant mortality rate was almost 58 deaths per 1,000 live births. The rate was estimated to be higher for males than for females—more than 62 male deaths per 1,000 live births, as compared with about 53 female deaths per 1,000 live births. Despite an increase of 14 years in the last decade, life expectancy at birth in Yemen has remained low compared with other developing countries— 60.6 years for males and 64.5 years for females, or 62.5 years overall. The country's fertility rate was almost 6.5 children per woman in 2007.

Ethnic Groups and Languages: Yemen's population is predominantly Arab, but it also includes Afro-Arabs, South Asians, and Europeans. Arabic is the official language; English is also used in official and business circles.

Religion: Virtually all of Yemen's citizens are Muslims; approximately 30 percent belong to the Zaydi sect of Shia Islam, and about 70 percent follow the Shafii school of Sunni Islam. A few thousand Ismaili Muslims, who adhere to Shia Islam, live in northern Yemen. Fewer than 500 Jews (a fraction of the former population) also live in the northern part of the country.

Yemen's constitution declares that Islam is the state religion and that the president of the republic must "practice his Islamic duties." The constitution also provides for freedom of religion, which the government generally respects but with limitations. The government prohibits the conversion and proselytizing of Muslims, requires permission for the construction of new places of worship, and permits non-Muslims to vote but not to hold elected office. Public schools provide instruction in Islam but not in other religions, although Muslim citizens are allowed to attend private schools that do not teach Islam. In an effort to curb ideological and religious extremism in schools, the government does not permit any courses outside of the officially approved curriculum to be taught in private and national schools. Because the government is concerned that unlicensed religious schools deviate from formal educational requirements and promote militant ideology, it has closed more than 4,500 of these institutions and deported foreign students studying there.

The free practice of religion has met with some government opposition. In 2004 the government used military force to quell an armed insurgency led by a Shia cleric in the northern governorate of Sadah. In March 2007, the government abolished the al-Haq political party, whose members are linked to this insurgency movement, citing the party's failure to meet political party law requirements. In early 2007, for the third year, the government banned the observance of a religious holiday that is celebrated there by some Shia Muslims and reportedly limited the hours that mosques were allowed to remain open, reassigned imams thought to espouse radical doctrine, and increased surveillance and detention of members of the insurgent group. According to the U.S. Department of State, Yemen's government, in an effort to curb extremism and increase tolerance, monitors mosques for inflammatory sermons and threatening political statements and uses police and intelligence agencies to screen the activities of Islamic organizations tied to international organizations.

Education and Literacy: According to composite data compiled by the World Bank, the adult literacy rate for Yemen in 2005 was 35 percent for females and 73 percent for males. The overall literacy rate for the population age 15 and older was 54 percent. By comparison, low-income countries in the aggregate average an adult literacy rate of almost 62 percent.

There is a direct correlation between the very high rate of illiteracy and the lack of basic education. Although Yemen's laws provide for universal, compulsory, free education for children ages six through 15, the U.S. Department of State reports that compulsory attendance is not enforced, and the cost of attendance (approximately US$10 per student per year) is an additional deterrent. This deficiency is confirmed by World Bank statistics. In 2006 only 75 percent of Yemen's school-age population was enrolled in primary school; enrollment was even lower for the female population—only 65 percent. In that same year, only 37 percent of the school-age population was enrolled in secondary school, including only 26 percent of eligible females. These low enrollment numbers are in turn a reflection of the countrywide shortage of the requisite infrastructure. School facilities and educational materials are of poor quality, classrooms are too few in number, and the teaching faculty is inadequate. In September 2004, the World Bank approved a US$121 million, six-year project to improve the quality of basic education (grades one through nine). Under this program, classroom facilities will be expanded and upgraded, curricula and educational materials improved, and the Ministry of Education's capacity to implement new programs and resources strengthened. In March 2008, the World Bank approved a US$103 million, seven-year project to improve gender equity, and the quality and efficiency of secondary education, focusing on girls in rural areas. This program, a major goal of which is to improve teaching and learning practices in the classroom, will upgrade school facilities and provide learning equipment as well as school community grants. Yemen's government has in recent years increased spending on education—from 4.5 percent of gross domestic product (GDP) in 1995 to 9.6 percent of GDP in 2005.

Health: Despite the significant progress Yemen has made to expand and improve its health care system over the past decade, the system remains severely underdeveloped. Total expenditures on health care in 2004 constituted 5 percent of gross domestic product. In that same year, the per capita expenditure for health care was very low compared with other Middle Eastern countries— US$34 according to the World Health Organization. According to the World Bank, the number of doctors in Yemen rose by an average of more than 7 percent between 1995 and 2000, but as of 2004 there were still only three doctors per 10,000 persons. In 2005 Yemen had only 6.1 hospital beds available per 10,000 persons.

Health care services are particularly scarce in rural areas; only 25 percent of rural areas are covered by health services, compared with 80 percent of urban areas. Emergency services, such as ambulance service and blood banks, are non-existent. Most childhood deaths are caused by illnesses for which vaccines exist or that are otherwise preventable. In 2003 an estimated 12,000 people in Yemen were living with human immunodeficiency virus/acquired immune deficiency syndrome (HIV/AIDS), according to the Joint United Nations Programme on HIV/AIDS.

Welfare: According to the United Nations, in 2005 Yemen ranked 153 out of 177 countries on the human development index (HDI), a measure of life expectancy, education, and standard of living. Yemen had the lowest HDI ranking among the Arab states. Several welfare programs are in place, but they generally have been considered inadequate to meet the needs of Yemen's impoverished citizens (estimated to exceed 45 percent of the total population). The main social assistance program is the Social Welfare Fund, initially established to compensate for reductions in economic subsidies. In 2006 this program provided 1 million beneficiaries direct cash payments capped at US$10 per month and lump-sum payments for emergencies. In March 2008, the government announced it would double the amount of cash transfers under this program and also increase retiree monthly pension benefits by US$7.50. The Social Fund for Development was established in 1997 with World Bank funds. Through its first and second phases, the fund has supported improved access of Yemen's poorest population to basic social services, and more effective and efficient delivery of social services. For the third phase, which is ongoing, the Bank provided US$60 million of International Development Association credit and in June 2007 approved an additional US$15 million. The three main components of this project are community development, capacity-building, and micro-financing programs.

ECONOMY

Overview: At the time of unification, South Yemen and North Yemen had vastly different but equally struggling underdeveloped economic systems. Since unification, the economy has been forced to sustain the consequences of Yemen's support for Iraq during the 1990–91 Gulf War: Saudi Arabia expelled almost 1 million Yemeni workers, and both Saudi Arabia and Kuwait significantly reduced economic aid to Yemen. The 1994 civil war further drained Yemen's economy. As a consequence, since 1995 Yemen has relied heavily on aid from multilateral agencies to sustain its economy. In return, it has pledged to implement significant economic reforms. In 1997 the International Monetary Fund (IMF) approved two programs to increase Yemen's credit significantly: the enhanced structural adjustment facility (now known as the poverty reduction and growth facility, or PRGF) and the extended funding facility (EFF). In the ensuing years, Yemen's government attempted, with limited success, to implement recommended reforms—reducing the civil service payroll, eliminating diesel and other subsidies, lowering defense spending, introducing a general sales tax, and privatizing state-run industries. As a result, Yemen has received only a fraction of the aid initially allocated by bilateral and multilateral lenders.

In late 2005, the World Bank, which, together with other lenders, had extended Yemen a four-year US$2.3 billion economic support package in October 2002, announced that, as a consequence of Yemen's failure to implement significant economic reforms and stem corruption, it would reduce financial aid by one-third, to US$280 million, over the period July 2005 through July 2008. Other funds pledged in the US$2.3 billion package were withheld as well. However, in May 2006 the World Bank adopted an assistance strategy for Yemen under which it will provide approximately US$400 million in International Development Association (IDA) credits over the period FY 2006 to FY 2009. In November 2006, Yemen's development partners pledged a total of US$5 billion in grants and concessional loans for the period 2007–10 to finance projects outlined in Yemen's five-year (2006–10) Development Plan for Poverty Reduction (DPPR). Recognizing that the country's oil reserves are rapidly depleting, the DPPR focuses on the development of the country's non-oil resources: natural gas, agriculture, fisheries, transshipment, and tourism. At a February 2008 meeting, international lenders in the Yemen Consultative Group announced that as of December 2007, 70 percent of the funds pledged (increased to US$5.3 billion) had been allocated. However, several attendees raised concerns about Yemen's lack of economic expansion, high population growth, worsening water crisis, and inability to contain security threats, all of which threaten to diminish the efficacy of international financial support. Yemen remains one of the poorest of the world's low-income countries; more than 45 percent of the population lives in poverty.

Gross Domestic Product (GDP): For 2006 Yemen's GDP was estimated to be US$19 billion. GDP per capita was estimated to be in a range of only US$880–US$904. World Bank and other economists have calculated a real growth rate of 3.2–4.0 percent in 2006, decreasing to a range of 2.8–3.6 percent in 2007, and estimate that real GDP growth in 2008 will remain unchanged. The general decline in the GDP growth rate is attributed to decreased oil production, which has negatively affected exports of goods and services, coupled with increased demand for imports. In the period 2008–9, however, the financial support pledged by bilateral and multilateral donors in November 2006 and the construction of a liquefied natural gas plant (expected to begin exports in early 2009) should offset the anticipated sharp decline in oil revenue, enabling GDP growth to remain constant. All of the rates estimated and forecast by economists fall far short of Yemen's five-year (2006–10) development plan, which calls for sustained average annual real GDP growth of 7 percent. The World Bank also has set a target of 7 percent GDP growth rate per year in order for Yemen to achieve sustained economic development.

Government Budget: In 1995, in order to comply with conditions stipulated by the International Monetary Fund, Yemen began an economic reform program, one component of which is fiscal policy reform aimed at reducing deficits and expanding the revenue base. However, the government has failed to significantly reduce its primary expenditure—subsidies, especially the fuel subsidy. Fuel subsidies accounted for an estimated 8.7 percent of gross domestic product (GDP) in 2007 and are forecast to rise to 11.8 percent of GDP in 2008. Coupled with the fuel subsidy, the government has continued to raise capital spending and increase civil service wages and pension benefits. Defense spending remains high, and in late 2007 the government adopted a supplementary US$1.3 billion budget to cover rising military costs stemming from internal security threats. Overall government spending is expected to increase by an annual average of approximately 14 percent in 2008–9. This trend has resulted in significant fiscal deficits—an estimated US$768 million in 2007 (3.7 percent of GDP) and US$1.2 billion in 2008 (4.9 percent of GDP); the deficit is forecast to reach US$2.3 billion in 2009.

Inflation: The implementation of economic reforms, including the cessation of Central Bank of Yemen financing of government budget deficits, reduced inflation from an average of 40 percent during the years immediately following unification (1990–96) to only 5.4 percent in 1997. High oil prices and cuts in the fuel subsidy brought the rate of inflation back up to an average of 11.4 percent from 2001 to 2004 and to 11.8 percent in 2005. Despite efforts by the Central Bank to contain the effects of both additional reductions in government fuel subsidies and the imposition of a general sales tax in 2005, the average annual inflation rate was 20.8 percent in 2006. Although inflation slowed sharply in the first half of 2007 as a result of lower prices for foodstuffs and intervention by the Central Bank, higher food prices in the latter part of 2007 pushed the annual average to 10 percent. Given increases in international non-oil commodity prices and strong domestic demand, economists project that the average inflation rate will reach 14.6 percent in 2008.

Agriculture, Forestry, and Fishing: Agriculture is the mainstay of Yemen's economy, generating more than 20 percent of gross domestic product (GDP) since 1990 (20.4 percent in 2005 according to the Central Bank of Yemen) and employing more than half (54.2 percent in 2003) of the working population. However, a U.S. government estimate suggests that the sector accounted for only 12.4 percent of GDP in 2007. Numerous environmental problems hamper growth in this sector—soil erosion, sand dune encroachment, and deforestation—but the greatest problem by far is the scarcity of water. As a result of low levels of rainfall, agriculture in Yemen relies heavily on the extraction of groundwater, a resource that is being depleted. Yemen's water tables are falling by approximately two meters a year. The use of irrigation has made fruit and vegetables Yemen's primary cash crops. With the rise in the output of irrigated crops, the production of traditional rain-fed crops such as cereals has declined. According to the Central Bank of Yemen, in 2005 the production of qat, a mildly narcotic and heavily cultivated plant that produces natural stimulants when its leaves are chewed, rose 6.7 percent and accounted for 5.8 percent of GDP; its usage in Yemen is widespread. According to the World Bank and other economists, cultivation of this plant plays a dominant role in Yemen's agricultural economy, constituting 10 percent of GDP and employing an estimated 150,000 persons while consuming an estimated 30 percent of irrigation water and displacing land areas that could otherwise be used for exportable coffee, fruits, and vegetables.

Although Yemen's extensive territorial waters and marine resources reportedly have the potential to produce 350,000–400,000 metric tons of fish each year, actual production is estimated to total only about 290,000 metric tons per year. The fishing industry is relatively underdeveloped and consists largely of individual fishermen in small boats. In recent years, the government has lifted restrictions on fish exports, and production has increased, yielding revenues valued at US$256 million in 2005. Fish and fish products constitute only 1.7 percent of Yemen's GDP but are the second largest export. In December 2005, the World Bank approved a US$25 million credit for a six-year Fisheries Management and Conservation Project to be launched in all coastal governorates along the Red Sea and the Gulf of Aden. This project is expected to improve fish landing and auction facilities, provide ice plants for fish preservation, and enable Yemen's Ministry of Fisheries to undertake more effective research, resource management planning, and regulatory activities.

Mining and Minerals: Yemen is a small oil producer and does not belong to the Organization of the Petroleum Exporting Countries (OPEC). Unlike many regional oil producers, Yemen relies heavily on foreign oil companies that have production-sharing agreements with the government. Income from oil production constitutes 75 percent of government revenue and about 85 percent of exports. Yemen had proven crude oil reserves of more than 3 billion barrels in 2007, down from 4 billion in 2006, and these reserves are not expected to last beyond 2020; in addition, output from the country's older fields is falling. According to statistics published by the U.S. Energy Information Administration, crude oil output averaged 380,000 barrels per day (bbl/d) in 2006, a reduction from 400,000 bbl/d in 2005. Crude oil output is projected to be 360,000 bbl/d in 2007 and to decrease to 350,000 bbl/d in 2008.

According to the *Oil and Gas Journal*, Yemen had 16.9 trillion cubic feet of proven natural gas reserves in 2007. Of this amount, 9 trillion cubic feet have been designated for the export of liquefied natural gas (LNG) by Yemen LNG (YLNG), which was formed in 1997 between Yemen Gas Company and various privately held companies. In July 2005, following years of setbacks, the government gave final approval to three LNG supply agreements, enabling YLNG to award a US$2.6 billion contract to an international consortium to build the country's first liquefaction plant at Balhat on the Arabian Sea coast. The plant is expected to deliver a total of 6.8 million tons of LNG per year; initial shipments are expected by early 2009, two-thirds for export to the United States and the remainder to Asia.

Industry and Manufacturing: The U.S. government estimates that Yemen's industrial sector constituted 40.9 percent of gross domestic product (GDP) in 2007. Together with services, construction, and commerce, industry accounts for less than 25 percent of the labor force. The largest contributor to the manufacturing sector's output is oil refining, which generates roughly 40 percent of total revenue. The remainder of this sector consists of the production of consumer goods and construction materials. Manufacturing constituted approximately 9.9 percent of Yemen's GDP in 2006. Almost all (95 percent) of the establishments are small businesses (one to four employees). Almost half of all industrial establishments are involved in processing food products and beverages; the production of flour and cooking oil has increased in recent years. Approximately 10 percent of the establishments are classified as manufacturing mixed metal products such as water-storage tanks, doors, and windows.

Energy: Yemen's state-owned Public Corporation for Electricity (PEC) operates an estimated 80 percent of the country's electricity generating capacity (1 gigawatt) as well as the national power grid. Over the past 10 years, the government has considered various means of alleviating the country's significant electricity shortage, including restructuring the PEC, integrating the power sector through small-scale privatization of power stations, creating independent power projects (IPPs), and introducing gas-generated power plants to free up oil supplies for export. In March 2005, Siemens signed a US$160 million contract to build a 340-megawatt gas-fueled power plant at Marib, with the potential to generate 1,000 megawatts. In November 2007, the Saudi Arabian government agreed to provide a US$101 million grant for this project. In May 2006, the World Bank approved a US$50 million loan to help finance the five-year Power Sector Project, which is designed to relieve critical power-sector supply constraints, enhance electricity supply efficiency and quality, and improve the efficiency of the PEC. In 2007 France's development financing agency, the Agence Française de Développement (AFD), gave Yemen a US$37 million concessional loan to help build capacity in the electricity sector.

In 2005 Yemen's diesel-run power plants generated 4.1 billion kilowatt-hours of electricity, a level of production that is insufficient to maintain a consistent supply of electricity. Although demand for electricity remains high, it is estimated that only 42 percent of the total population has access to electricity from the national power grid, and supply is intermittent, with frequent blackouts. To meet this demand, the government plans to increase the country's power generating capacity an additional 1,400 megawatts by 2010.

Services: International economists have reported that Yemen's services sector constituted 52.6 percent of gross domestic product (GDP) in 2004 and 53.1 percent of GDP in 2005. The U.S. government estimates that the services sector accounted for 46.7 percent of GDP in 2007.

Banking and Finance: Yemen's financial services sector is underdeveloped and dominated by the banking system. Yemen has no public stock exchange, but the government wants to establish one by 2011. The banking system consists of the Central Bank of Yemen, 16 commercial banks (nine private domestic banks, four of which are Islamic banks; five private foreign banks; and two state-owned banks), and two specialized state-owned development banks. The Central Bank of Yemen controls monetary policy and oversees the transfer of currencies abroad. It is the lender of last resort, exercises supervisory authority over commercial banks, and serves as a banker to the government. The largest commercial bank, the National Bank of Yemen, which is fully state-owned, and the Yemen Bank for Reconstruction and Development, which is majority state-owned, are currently being restructured with the goal of eventual privatization. Because of fiscal difficulties in both banks, in 2004 Yemen's government approved a plan to merge them, but no action has been taken.

The large volume of non-performing loans, low capitalization, and weak enforcement of regulatory standards hamper Yemen's banking sector as a whole. Numerous banks are technically insolvent. Because many debtors are in default, Yemen's banks limit their lending activities to a select group of consumers and businesses; as a result, the entire banking system holds less than 60 percent of the money supply. The bulk of the economy operates with cash. Legislation adopted in 2000 gave the Central Bank the authority to enforce tougher lending requirements, and in mid-2005 the Central Bank promulgated several new capital requirements for commercial banks aimed at curtailing currency speculation and protecting deposits. In 2007 Yemen's banking law was amended to ease entry conditions for foreign banks and strengthen the oversight of Islamic banks. In March 2008, Yemen's parliament approved legislation establishing an independent deposit insurance agency to protect depositors with assets of US$10,000 or less.

Tourism: Yemen's tourism industry is hampered by limited infrastructure as well as serious security concerns. The country's hotels and restaurants are below international standards, and air and road transportation is largely inadequate. Kidnappings of foreign tourists remain a threat, especially outside the main cities, and, coupled with attacks on foreigners in 2007 and early 2008, present a significant deterrent to tourism. In April 2008, the U.S. Department of State reiterated previous warnings to U.S. citizens, urging them to defer non-essential travel to Yemen because the security threat level remains high. In March 2008, Britain's Foreign Office issued a similar advisory. Recent statistics for tourist arrivals in Yemen are not available, but in 2005 the number rose to 336,000 from 274,000 in 2004.

Labor: According to the U.S. government, the agriculture and herding sector employs the majority of Yemen's working population (54.2 percent in 2003). Industry, together with services, construction, and commerce, accounts for less than 25 percent of the labor force. The country's unemployment rate is estimated to be 35 percent.

According to the World Bank and other economists, Yemen's civil service is characterized by a large, poorly paid workforce, multiple salary structures, and an absence of effective enforcement measures to counter fraud. As the government has sought to appease discontent over a stagnant economy, civil service salaries have increased dramatically—doubling between 2000 and 2005. The 2005 budget reduced economic subsidies but in exchange required the government to make various concessions, including increasing civil service wages another 10 to 15 percent by 2007 as part of a national wage strategy.

In 2006 the government provided across-the-board wage increases as the first phase of a four-phase Civil Service Modernization Project. The second phase was implemented in November 2007, providing an average 20 percent salary increase for all public-sector employees at an estimated cost of US$402 million. In March 2008, the government announced a US$15 per month increase in civil service and military personnel salaries. A major reform underway is the implementation of a biometric identification system for civilian and military personnel by September 2008; it is designed to eliminate the collection of multiple salaries by one employee. The Ministry of Civil Services is also developing other procedural reforms. The International Monetary Fund has stated that Yemen must reduce civil service salaries as a component of GDP, but this goal can be achieved only with continued reductions in the size of the civil service.

Foreign Economic Relations: During the 1990–91 Gulf War, Yemen supported Iraq in its invasion of Kuwait, thereby alienating Saudi Arabia and Kuwait, both of which had provided critical financial assistance to Yemen. In addition to withdrawing this aid, Saudi Arabia expelled almost 1 million Yemeni workers. The resultant fall in expatriate remittances had a disastrous impact on Yemen's governmental budget. The civil war of 1994 further drained the economy, and in 1995 Yemen sought the aid of multilateral agencies. In 1996 the International Monetary Fund (IMF) granted Yemen a US$190 million stand-by credit facility, and the following year it approved two funding facilities that increased the country's credit by approximately US$500 million. However, the funding was contingent on Yemen's adoption of stringent economic reforms, a requirement that the country had limited success in fulfilling. As a result, the IMF suspended lending to Yemen from late 1999 until February 2001. In 2000 Kuwait and Saudi Arabia resumed financial aid to Yemen.

In October 2002, bilateral and multilateral lenders led by the World Bank agreed to give Yemen a four-year economic support package worth US$2.3 billion, 20 percent in grants and 80 percent in concessional loans. This funding is almost eight times the amount of financial support Yemen received from the IMF. However, in December 2005 the World Bank announced that because of the government's continued inability to effect significant economic reforms and stem corruption, funding would be reduced by more than one-third, from US$420 million to US$280 million for the period July 2005–July 2008. In May 2006, the World Bank adopted a new Country Assistance Strategy (CAS) for Yemen for the period FY 2006 to FY 2009, providing a blueprint for fostering the country's fiscal and human development improvement. The bank pledged to contribute approximately US$400 million in International Development Association (IDA) credits over the CAS time frame. In December 2005, the Japanese government pledged to write off US$17 million of the US$264 Yemen owes. That same month, Germany pledged to increase its annual aid to Yemen to US$83.6 million over the next two years; funding will go primarily to education and water improvement projects. In November 2006, the United Kingdom announced that aid to Yemen would increase 400 percent, to US$222 million through 2011. In June 2008, the Yemeni General Investment Authority and the Chinese Council for the Promotion of International Trade jointly convened a symposium to advance the already strong trade and investment relationship between the two countries. During this meeting, China announced that it would provide a US$12 million grant to support development projects in Yemen.

Yemen is a member of the Arab Fund for Economic and Social Development, which since 1974 has contributed to the financing of economic and social development in Arab states and countries through loans and guarantees. In March 2004, the Arab League provided US$136 million to Yemen to finance infrastructure improvements. At a mid-November 2006 meeting in London, a group of bilateral and multilateral donors pledged US$5 billion over four years (2007–10) to fund economic development in Yemen. The goal of the meeting, which was jointly chaired by the World Bank and the government of Yemen, was to provide sufficient economic aid to Yemen to enable it to qualify for future Gulf Cooperation Council (GCC) membership. More than 55 percent of the aid, which is primarily in the form of grants and has been increased to US$5.3 billion, will come from the GCC. In December 2007, the United Arab Emirates raised its pledge from US$500 million to US$650 million. Yemen was granted observer status at the World Trade Organization (WTO) in 1999, and its application for full membership is currently under negotiation.

Imports: Imports totaled US$4.7 billion in 2006, increased to an estimated US$6.7 billion in 2007, and are projected to increase to US$7.5 billion in 2008. This increase is due in part to Yemen's reliance on foreign capital goods for its gas and infrastructure programs. Yemen is a net importer of all major categories of products except fuels. Principal imports are machinery and transport equipment, food and livestock, and processed materials. The principal source of Yemen's imports in 2006 was the United Arab Emirates (15.8 percent of total imports); the bulk of these imports are actually re-exports from industrialized countries. Yemen received 12.3 percent of its total imports from China and 7.5 percent from Saudi Arabia.

Exports: In 2006 Yemen's exports totaled US$7.3 billion. Crude oil is Yemen's main export, accounting for 85 percent of total exports in 2006. Yemen's non-oil exports are primarily agricultural products, mainly fish and fish products and coffee. In 2006 Asia remained the most important market for Yemen's exports, primarily China (29.9 percent of total exports), India, Thailand, and South Korea.

Trade Balance: Yemen's import and export values have increased and decreased dramatically in the past 10 years owing to shifts in global oil prices. As a result, the country's trade balance has fluctuated significantly from a deficit of almost US$800 million in 1998 to a surplus of US$1 billion in 2000. Rising oil prices resulted in a surplus of US$1.7 billion in 2005. The Central Bank of Yemen estimates that the trade surplus reached US$2.6 billion (about 13.3 percent of gross domestic product) in 2006.

Balance of Payments: In recent years, Yemen's large non-merchandise deficits have contributed to a decline in its current-account position. Up until 2007, these deficits were offset by record export earnings, which resulted in large enough trade surpluses to keep the current account in surplus—US$633.2 million in 2005 and US$1.8 billion in 2006. In 2007, however, the rise in import spending resulted in an estimated current-account deficit of US$519 million, the first such deficit for Yemen since 1998. This deficit is projected to increase to US$660 million in 2008.

External Debt: In 1990 the newly unified Republic of Yemen inherited an unsustainable debt burden amounting to roughly 106 percent of gross domestic product. Debt rescheduling by the Paris Club creditor countries in the 1990s, coupled with assistance from the World Bank's International Development Agency, resulted in a drop in Yemen's debt stock to US$5.4 billion in 2006. According to the Central Bank of Yemen, Yemen's debt stock was US$5.8 billion (more than 25 percent of gross domestic product) by year-end 2007. According to the U.S. government, Yemen's reserves of foreign exchange and gold were US$7.9 billion in 2007.

Foreign Investment: Yemen does not have a stock exchange, therefore limiting inward portfolio investment. Portfolio investment abroad is also very limited, with the result that portfolio flows are largely unrecorded by authorities. In the early 1990s, net direct investment was at its peak as foreign investors tapped Yemeni oil reserves, but since 1995 net direct investment flows have been negative because cost recovery for foreign oil companies has exceeded new direct investment. A US$3 billion liquid natural gas (LNG) construction project involving a consortium of foreign companies is underway following government approval in August 2005, with initial exports expected in early 2009. Such a project raises the prospect of increased foreign investment in the future as LNG facilities are built.

Currency and Exchange Rate: Yemen's currency is the Yemeni riyal (YR), which was floated on the open market in July 1996. Periodic intervention by the Central Bank of Yemen enabled the riyal to gradually depreciate approximately 4.2 percent per year from 1999 to 2003, and in varying amounts in subsequent years. However, in light of the weakening U.S. dollar, and in an effort to stem inflation, in 2007 the Central Bank of Yemen halted the riyal's depreciation. Its value averaged YR191.5 per US$1 in 2005, YR197 per US$1 in 2006, and YR 199 per US$1 in 2007. The exchange rate is expected to continue to average YR 199 per US$1 in 2008. In mid-August 2008, the exchange rate was nearly YR 200 per US$1. (EIU 2007, April 2008; Central Bank of Yemen))

Fiscal Year: Yemen's fiscal year coincides with the calendar year.

TRANSPORTATION AND TELECOMMUNICATIONS

Overview: As a direct consequence of its poverty, Yemen compares unfavorably with its Middle Eastern neighbors in terms of transportation infrastructure and communications network. Roads are generally poor, but several projects are planned to upgrade the system. Although there is no rail network, a rail line linking Yemen with Oman is under consideration by the Gulf Cooperation Council. Efforts to upgrade airport facilities have languished, and telephone and Internet usage and capabilities are limited. The port of Aden has shown a promising recovery from a 2002 attack; container throughput increased significantly in 2006 and set a record level in 2007. However, the agreement to turn over long-term management of the port's main facility, Aden Container Terminal, to DP World has become controversial and is not yet finalized.

Roads: Relative to Yemen's size, the road transportation system is very limited. Yemen has 71,300 kilometers of roads, only 6,200 kilometers of which are paved. In the north, roads connecting Sanaa, Taizz, and Al Hudaydah are good, as are intercity bus services. In the south, roads are generally poor and in need of repair, except for the Aden–Taizz road. In November 2005, the World Bank approved a five-year, almost US$50 million project to upgrade approximately 200 kilometers of intermediate rural roads and approximately 75 kilometers of village access roads as part of a larger effort to strengthen Yemen's capability for rural road planning and engineering. Plans are well advanced to build an estimated US$1.6 billion highway linking Aden in the south and Amran in the north. The road will include more than 10 tunnels and halve the travel time between the southern seacoast and the northern border with Saudi Arabia.

Railroads: Yemen has no rail network, but a regional rail network planned by the Gulf Cooperation Council states is expected to include a 1,000-kilometer rail line linking Muscat, Oman, with the eastern Yemeni border outpost Shihen (also seen as Shahan). Under the supervision of the World Bank, three international consultancies have been preparing feasibility studies for this project since September 2007; their findings are expected by the end of 2008.

Ports: Yemen's main ports are Aden, Al Hudaydah, Al Mukalla, and Mocha; Aden is the primary port. In addition, Ras Isa serves as the loading point for oil exports, and a small amount of cargo passes through Nishtun.

Facilities at Aden consist of the Maalla Terminal and the Aden Container Terminal (ACT), which opened in March 1999. The port can handle roll-on-roll-off and container cargoes, as well as tankers. In November 2003, following the October 2002 bombing of the French supertanker *Limburg* off the Yemen coast and the resultant dramatic drop in throughput at the Aden port, the Port of Singapore Authority sold its majority stake in the ACT back to the Yemeni government. In June 2005, Dubai Ports International (later renamed DP World) was selected to upgrade and operate the ACT under a 35-year contract, but Yemen's parliament refused to approve the deal. Acknowledging both the wealth of DP World and the United Arab Emirates' strong economic support, in 2007 the Yemeni government resumed contract negotiations with DP World. Pending agreement on a final contract, which remains uncertain, Aden Gulf Seaports Corporation, a government entity, is managing the port. The port of Aden has recovered well from the 2002 bombing. In 2005 the port handled 317,897 twenty-foot-equivalent units (TEUs) of containers, slightly more than double the amount for 2003. The port handled 397,080 TEUs of containers in 2006 and a record 503,325 TEUs of containers in 2007.

Inland Waterways: Yemen has no waterways of any significant length.

Civil Aviation and Airports: Yemen has 50 airports, 17 of which have paved runways. Of the 50 airports, four are international—Aden International, Sanaa International, Taizz, and Al Hudaydah. A major reconstruction and expansion of Aden International was completed in 2001, including a new runway that can handle large, long-haul aircraft. Plans to make that airport a regional cargo hub, with an "air cargo village," by 2004 have all but failed. Although construction began in January 2003, by year's end the managing company had dissolved. In December 2006, the chairman of the Aden Free Zone announced that US$250 million of funds allocated to Yemen at the November London donors' conference would be directed to this project.

Yemenia is the national airline; it absorbed the former national carrier of South Yemen in 1996. It is expected that Yemenia, which is currently 49 percent owned by the Saudi government and 51 percent by the Yemen government, will eventually be privatized, but there has been resistance from the Saudis. In 2001 the airline carried 858,000 passengers. Because the airline's existing fleet of 12 aircraft is rapidly becoming outdated, in 2002 three new aircraft were leased for eight years, and in early 2006 the airline announced plans to acquire six new aircraft, with options for an additional four, beginning in 2012. In May 2006, the company allocated US$2 million for upgrades, including electronic ticketing and reservations.

Pipelines: According to the U.S. government, as of 2007 Yemen had a total of 1,402 kilometers of pipelines. This total includes pipeline designed for gas (71 kilometers), liquid petroleum gas (22 kilometers), and oil (1,309 kilometers).

Telecommunications: TeleYemen is the exclusive provider of international telecommunications for Yemen—fixed-line, telex, and Internet services—and is one of the mobile-phone operators. In 2003 the government-owned Public Telecommunications Corporation assumed full control of TeleYemen, and a year later it awarded a five-year management contract to France Telecom.

According to the U.S. government, Yemen had only 270,000 Internet users in 2006. This low number is attributed to the high cost of computer equipment and connections in combination with the population's low level of income, as well as to the restricted bandwidth available on Yemen's outdated telephone network. In 2005 TeleYemen announced it would invest in the FALCON high-capacity loop cable system, which will improve Internet access, including broadband capability, and also expand international call accessibility.

The cost of running a landline or owning a mobile telephone is out of reach for most of Yemen's poor population, resulting in very low telephone usage rates—3.9 fixed-line subscribers and 9.5 mobile subscribers per 100 persons in 2005. The U.S. government reported 968,400 landlines and 2 million mobile subscribers in Yemen in 2006. The technology used for domestic lines includes microwave radio relay, cable, and Global System for Mobile Communications (GSM). In 2001 two private companies won 15-year licenses to provide mobile phone services. The growth of the companies' networks has resulted in coverage of about 60 percent of the population, but threats to internal security coupled with poor consumer payment history remain obstacles to future growth. In August 2005, the government awarded a contract to a joint venture between China Mobile and a group of Yemeni investors to take a 55 percent stake in Yemen's third mobile network; the government will retain a 25 percent share. In August 2006, the same conglomerate was awarded a contract for a fourth mobile network.

The state-run Republic of Yemen Television and Republic of Yemen Radio operate the country's television and radio networks, respectively. According to the U.S. government, as of 1998

17

Yemen had six AM, one FM, and two shortwave radio broadcast stations and, as of 2007, three television broadcast stations, plus several low-power repeaters.

GOVERNMENT AND POLITICS

Political System/Overview: Since unification in 1990, Yemen has officially been a republic. According to the constitution, "the political system of the Republic of Yemen is based on political and partisan pluralism." In reality, however, the General People's Congress (GPC), which is headed by President Ali Abdallah Salih (who won re-election in September 2006 with 77 percent of the vote), dominates the government and continues to hold an absolute majority in parliament as a result of the 2003 elections. In 2001 several constitutional amendments, passed by national referendum, strengthened the powers of the executive branch. The president was given the authority to dissolve parliament without a national referendum, and his term of office was extended to seven years. The Shura Council appointed by the president was almost doubled in size and given enhanced legislative authority. Yemen's judiciary is perceived as weak and corrupt, and numerous government efforts to effect reform have as yet failed to improve the functioning of the judicial system. In April 2007, a presidential decree was issued declaring the appointment of a new prime minister and Council of Ministers. The ministerial changes were made in response to concerns about Yemen's declining economy and allegations of corruption. In October 2007, President Salih announced several constitutional reform measures designed to democratize Yemen's political system and empower local authorities, but the prospect for their implementation remains uncertain.

Constitution: Yemen's constitution was ratified by popular referendum on May 16, 1991. It defines the republic as an independent and sovereign Arab and Islamic country and establishes sharia, or Islamic law, as the basis of all laws. In February 2001, several amendments were passed by national referendum extending the presidential term to seven years and the parliamentary term to six years and increasing the size and authority of the Shura Council.

Branches of Government: Yemen's current president, Ali Abdallah Salih, was reelected by universal suffrage in September 2006 for a seven-year term. He won the election with 77 percent of the vote, despite a challenge from the opposition Joint Meeting Parties (JMP) coalition candidate, Faisal bin Shamlan. The president appoints a vice president and a prime minister, who in turn appoints the 35-member Council of Ministers. Yemen's legislature is bicameral, composed of an elected 301-seat House of Representatives (parliament) and an appointed Shura Council with 111 members. The parliament, whose members serve six-year terms, enacts laws, sanctions general state policy and the socioeconomic plan, and approves government budgets and final accounts. The current parliament is dominated by the ruling party, the General People's Congress; as a result, it has failed to initiate legislation, instead debating policies that the government submits, and is generally perceived as an ineffective check on executive-branch authority. Pursuant to 2001 constitutional amendments, the Shura Council, whose role is primarily advisory, has the power to vote jointly with parliament on any legislative matters of the president's choice.

Yemen has six types of courts: criminal, civil, personal status, special cases (e.g., kidnaping, carjacking, and acts of sabotage), commercial, and court-martial. In recent years, other limited-jurisdiction courts, e.g., juvenile and public funds courts, have been established under executive authority. The judicial system is organized in a three-tiered court structure. At the base are the courts of first instance, with broad powers to hear all manner of civil, criminal, commercial, and family matters. At the next level are the courts of appeal, one in each governorate and one in Sanaa. Each court of appeal has separate divisions for criminal, military, civil, and family issues. The highest court, the Supreme Court, settles jurisdictional disputes between courts, hears cases brought against high government officials, serves as the final court of appeal for all lower court decisions, and determines the constitutionality of laws and regulations. In addition to this formal court system, there is a system of tribal adjudication. It is responsible primarily for non-criminal issues, but in practice these courts adjudicate criminal cases as well.

Administrative Divisions: Yemen is divided into 19 governorates. According to the U.S. government, for electoral and administrative purposes the capital city of Sanaa is treated as an additional governorate. A United Nations report on the preliminary results of Yemen's 2004 population census also lists Raimah as a new governorate.

Provincial and Local Government: Formal government authority is centralized in the capital city of Sanaa. Yemen's Local Authority Law decentralized authority by establishing locally elected district and governorate councils (last elected in September 2006), formerly headed by government-appointed governors. After the September 2006 local and governorate council elections, President Salih announced various measures that would enable future governors and directors of the councils to be directly elected. In May 2008, governors were elected for the first time. However, because the ruling party, the General People's Congress (GPC), continues to dominate the local and governorate councils, the May 2008 elections retained this party's executive authority over the governorates. In rural Yemen, direct state control is weak, with tribal confederations acting as autonomous sub-states.

Judicial and Legal System: Yemen's constitution, as amended, stipulates that Islamic law (sharia) is the source of all legislation. All laws are based on a combination of sharia, old Egyptian laws, and Napoleonic tradition. Defendants are presumed innocent until proven guilty; indigent defendants in felony cases are by law entitled to counsel, but in practice this does not always occur. Trials, which are generally public, are conducted without juries; judges adjudicate criminal cases. All defendants have the right of appeal. Women often suffer discrimination, particularly in domestic matters.

Although Yemen's constitution provides for an autonomous judiciary and independent judges, in reality the judiciary is managed by an executive-branch council, the Supreme Judicial Council (SJC), and judges are appointed and can be removed by the executive branch. The judicial system itself is considered weak; corruption is widespread; the government is often reluctant to enforce judgments; and judges are subject to harassment from tribal leaders, who themselves exercise significant discretion in the interpretation and application of the law. There have been several restructurings of the judiciary since the government initiated a judicial reform program in 1997, but none have resulted in any significant improvements in the functioning of the system or produced evidence of having reduced corruption.

Electoral System: Yemen has universal suffrage for those age 18 and older. The constitution provides that the president be elected by popular vote from at least two candidates endorsed by parliament. In 1999 the first nationwide direct presidential election was held, giving Ali Abdallah Salih, the leader of the General People's Congress (GPC), a five-year term, which was extended to seven years in 2001. President Salih was reelected in September 2006 with 77 percent of the popular vote. The electorate also elects the parliament every six years, most recently in April 2003. The next parliamentary elections are to be held in April 2009. Although the various 2006 elections (presidential and local) were deemed by international observers to be generally open and competitive, there were reports of irregularities, such as underage and duplicate voting and the use of state funds to support GPC candidates.

Politics and Political Parties: Yemen's Political Parties Law mandates that political parties be viable national organizations comprising at least 75 founders and 2,500 members and not restrict membership to a particular region. The government provides financial support to political parties, including a stipend for newspaper publication. The ruling party, the General People's Congress (GPC), captured 238 of 301 seats in parliament in the 2003 elections. In the September 2006 elections for local and governorate councils, the GPC garnered 315 seats in the governorates (74 percent of the popular vote) and 5,078 local council seats (74 percent of the popular vote). In 2005 a coalition of five opposition parties formed the Joint Meeting Parties (JMP) to effect political and economic reform. The JMP includes the northern-based, tribal, and Islamist-oriented Yemeni Congregation for Reform (Islah) and the secular Yemeni Socialist Party (YSP), which represents the remnants of the former South Yemeni leadership. In the September 2006 presidential election, the JMP backed opposition candidate Faisal bin Shamlan, whose success in garnering 22 percent of the popular vote was viewed at the time as a first step in challenging the political stronghold of President Salih and the GPC. However, disputes between the GPC and the JMP in 2007 over election law amendments, coupled with the JMP's opposition to President Salih's proposed democratic reform measures, have halted initial attempts to forge a dialogue between the two parties.

Mass Media: Yemen's Ministry of Information influences the media through its control of printing presses, granting of newspaper subsidies, and ownership of the country's only television and radio stations. According to the U.S. Department of State, Yemen has nine government-controlled, 50 independent, and 30 party-affiliated newspapers. There are approximately 90 magazines, 50 percent of which are private, 30 percent government-controlled, and 20 percent party-affiliated. The government controls the content of news broadcasts and rarely permits antigovernment material to be aired. Although Yemen's government claims it does not monitor Internet usage, the U.S. Department of State reports that the government does occasionally block political and religious Web sites. By law and regulation, newspapers and magazines must be government-licensed, and their content is restricted. There have been reports of journalists being physically attacked, as well as arrested and detained.

Foreign Relations: The 1990–91 Gulf War had a significant negative impact on Yemen's relations with its Arab neighbors. As a member of the United Nations Security Council during those years, Yemen abstained on a number of Security Council resolutions concerning Iraq and Kuwait, did not support economic sanctions against Iraq, and called for an "Arab solution" to the crisis. Western and neighboring Gulf states responded by curtailing or canceling aid programs and diplomatic contacts. In particular, Saudi Arabia and Kuwait cut off critical financial aid and budgetary support, and Saudi Arabia expelled almost 1 million Yemeni workers, all of which had a profound impact on Yemen's government finances. Yemen did not succeed in re-establishing diplomatic ties with Kuwait until 1999; in 2000, when a border agreement was signed with Saudi Arabia, Kuwait agreed to resume financial aid. The treaty Yemen signed with Saudi Arabia resolved a 50-year-old dispute between the two countries, providing coordinates for delineating the land and maritime border. In 1995 Yemen and Oman finalized the demarcation of their common border and currently have a strong trade relationship. Yemen's long-term goal is membership in the Gulf Cooperation Council (GCC), and its foreign policy is largely driven by its desire to secure the financial support of GCC member states. At a meeting of international donors in November 2006, the largest block of aid to Yemen, US$1 billion, was pledged by Saudi Arabia.

Although relations with the West were strained as a result of Yemen's pro-Iraq stance during the first Gulf War, ties were re-established by the mid-1990s when Western democracies urged the International Monetary Fund (IMF) and the World Bank to extend financial assistance to Yemen. In 1999 the United States began using Aden as a refueling stop for the U.S. Navy. After the October 2000 bombing of the USS *Cole* in that harbor, Yemen strengthened its efforts against the Islamist groups responsible for the attack. In July 2001, the United States renewed the bilateral financial aid that had been frozen since the Gulf War. Since September 11, 2001, relations between Yemen and the United States are considered to be significantly stronger. Yemen reportedly values the military and financial support the United States provides, as well as its influence with the IMF, which has serious concerns about Yemen's commitment to economic reform. According to the U.S. Department of State, as of late 2007 the United States considered Yemen an important partner in the global war on terrorism, providing assistance in the military, diplomatic, and financial arenas. The U.S. government reaffirmed its commitment to provide economic and military support to Yemen during November 2005 and May 2007 meetings between the White House and President Salih. However, in April 2008 the United States embassy in Sanaa was the potential target of a mortar attack. This incident, coupled with Yemen's refusal to extradite two al Qaeda suspects convicted in Yemen of terrorist attacks, has strained relations between Yemen and the United States.

Membership in International Organizations: Yemen is a member of the United Nations (UN) and many of its affiliates and specialized agencies: Food and Agriculture Organization, International Civil Aviation Organization, International Fund for Agricultural Development, International Labour Organization, International Maritime Organization, International Telecommunication Union, UN Conference on Trade and Development, UN Educational, Scientific and Cultural Organization, UN High Commissioner for Refugees, UN Industrial Development Organization, Universal Postal Union, and World Health Organization. Yemen is also a member of the Arab Fund for Economic and Social Development, Arab Monetary Fund, Council of Arab Economic Unity, Group of 77, International Atomic Energy Agency, International Bank for Reconstruction and Development, International Civil Aviation Organization, International Confederation of Free Trade Unions, International Criminal Court (signatory), International Criminal Police Organization, International Federation of Red Cross and Red Crescent Societies, International Finance Corporation, International Monetary Fund, Islamic Development Bank, League of Arab States, Multilateral Investment Guarantee Investment Agency, Organisation for the Prohibition of Chemical Weapons, Organization of the

Islamic Conference, World Intellectual Property Organization, and World Meteorological Organization. Yemen was granted observer status at the World Trade Organization (WTO) in 1999 and in 2002 and 2003 submitted necessary documentation for full membership. The WTO working party on Yemen met in 2004 and twice thereafter to discuss Yemen's accession; negotiations are expected to take several years.

Major International Treaties: Yemen is a signatory to various international agreements on agricultural commodities, commerce, defense, economic and technical cooperation, finance, and postal matters. Yemen is a Non-Annex I country under the United Nations Framework Convention on Climate Change. Yemen is not a signatory to the Kyoto Protocol but has acceded to it, which has the same legal effect as ratification. Yemen is a signatory to the Nuclear Non-Proliferation Treaty, a party to the Biological Weapons Convention, and has signed and ratified the Chemical Weapons Convention. Yemen is also a party to environmental conventions on Biodiversity, Desertification, Environmental Modification, Hazardous Wastes, Law of the Sea, and Ozone Layer Protection.

NATIONAL SECURITY

Armed Forces Overview: The armed forces of the Yemen Arab Republic and the People's Democratic Republic of Yemen were officially merged in May 1990, but in May 1994 civil war broke out between the forces of the two former states, culminating in victory for the North. In October 1994, President Ali Abdallah Salih announced plans for the modernization of the armed forces, which would include the banning of party affiliation in the security services and armed forces, and in March 1995 the full merger of the armed forces was completed. The number of military personnel in Yemen is relatively high; in sum, Yemen has the second largest military force on the Arabian Peninsula after Saudi Arabia. Yemen's military consists of an army, navy, air force, and reserves. In 2007 total active troops were estimated as follows: army, 60,000; navy, 1,700; and air force, 5,000. In September 2007, the government announced the reinstatement of compulsory military service. Yemen's defense budget, which in 2006 represented approximately 40 percent of the total government budget, is expected to remain high for the near term, as the military draft takes effect and internal security threats continue to escalate. Despite these troop levels, Yemen's military equipment is considered to be light, outdated, and poorly maintained, particularly when compared with neighboring Gulf states.

Foreign Military Relations: Although no U.S. troops are based permanently in Yemen, the United States has provided military assistance and technical support in recent years. According to the U.S. Department of State, the resumption of International Military Education and Training (IMET) assistance and the transfer of military equipment and spare parts to Yemen have improved defense relations between the United States and Yemen. In FY 2006, Foreign Military Financing for Yemen was US$8.4 million, IMET was US$924,000, and Non-Proliferation, Anti-Terrorism, Demining and Related Programs received US$1.4 million. Nongovernment sources report that in addition to this aid, U.S. military advisers have trained Yemeni troops in counterterrorism techniques, and the United States has contributed to Yemen's border security by installing advanced technological immigration control systems. In an effort to bolster Yemen's maritime security and establish a coast guard capable of stemming terrorist activities, the United States has sent naval experts to train the new Yemeni coast guard and in 2004–5 donated 14 patrol craft to the coast guard. In 2005 an Australian company delivered 10 patrol boats to assist Yemeni government efforts to combat terrorism and illegal trafficking; the company will train crews to man the vessels.

External Threat: In the aftermath of the 1990–91 Gulf War when Yemen sided with Iraq in its invasion of Kuwait, both Kuwait and Saudi Arabia broke diplomatic ties with Yemen. Although these ties have been restored, tensions remain over the Saudi Arabia–Yemen border; in early 2008, Saudi Arabia reinforced its concrete-filled security barrier along sections of the border in order to stem illegal cross-border activities. Despite increased border security, fugitive Islamist militants from throughout the Gulf region, especially Saudi Arabia, Afghanistan, and Iraq, regularly cross what is still perceived as a lax border into Yemen. This poses a security threat to a country battling terrorism on many fronts.

Defense Budget: Yemen's defense spending has historically been one of the government's three largest expenditures and is expected to remain high as a result of the reinstatement of conscription and security threats posed by terrorism and tribal conflict. The defense budget increased from US$540 million in 2001 to and estimated US$823 million–US$1.1 billion in 2006. According to the U.S. government, the 2006 budget represents about 6 percent of gross domestic product.

Major Military Units: Yemen's military is divided into an army, navy, and air force. The army is organized into eight armored brigades, 16 infantry brigades, six mechanized brigades, two airborne commando brigades, one surface-to-surface missile brigade, three artillery brigades, one central guard force, one Special Forces brigade, and six air defense brigades, which consist of four antiaircraft artillery battalions and one surface-to-air missile battalion. The navy's major bases are located in Aden and Al Hudaydah; there are also bases in Al Mukalla, Perim Island, and Socotra that maintain naval support equipment. The air force includes an air defense force.

Major Military Equipment: Yemen's army is reported to be equipped with 790 main battle tanks, 130 reconnaissance vehicles, 200 armored infantry fighting vehicles, 710 armored personnel carriers, 310 towed artillery, 25 self-propelled artillery, 294 multiple rocket launchers, 502 mortars, six Scud B (up to an estimated 33 missiles) and 28 other surface-to-surface missiles, 71 antitank guided weapons, some rocket launchers, some recoilless launchers, 530 air defense guns, and an estimated 800 surface-to-air missiles. The navy's inventory includes eight missile craft, six miscellaneous boats/craft, five inshore patrol craft, six mine countermeasures vessels, one landing ship (tank), two landing craft (mechanical), four landing craft (utility), and two support and miscellaneous tankers. The air force, including air defense, has 75 combat aircraft and eight attack helicopters, as well as assorted transport aircraft, training aircraft and helicopters, and both air-to-air and air-to-surface missiles.

Military Service: In 2001 Yemen's National Defense Council abolished the existing two-year compulsory military service, relying instead on volunteers to fill posts in the military and security forces. In 2007 the government announced it would reinstate the draft to counter unemployment; approximately 70,000 new recruits are expected to join the military.

23

Paramilitary Forces: Yemen's paramilitary force has about 71,000 troops. Approximately 50,000 constitute the Central Security Organization of the Ministry of Interior; they are equipped with a range of infantry weapons and armored personnel carriers. An additional 20,000 are forces of armed tribal levies. Yemen is building up a small coast guard under the Ministry of Interior, training naval military technicians for posts in Aden and Al Mukalla. The coast guard currently has 1,200 personnel.

Foreign Military Forces: There are no permanent U.S. troops in Yemen, but military personnel have been deployed there in recent years for training purposes. Since the February 2006 escape of 23 Al Qaeda members from a prison in Sanaa, an international coalition of warships has patrolled the waterways off Yemen.

Military Forces Abroad: Yemen's Middle Eastern neighbors who are members of the Gulf Cooperation Council (GCC) participate in a defense force based in Saudi Arabia. Yemen is not a member of the GCC, and there are no reports of the country having a military presence outside of its own borders.

Police: Yemen's primary and most feared internal security and intelligence-gathering force is the Political Security Organization (PSO), led by military officers; it reports directly to the president and operates its own detention centers. There are an estimated 150,000 personnel in the PSO. The Central Security Organization, which is part of the Ministry of Interior, maintains a paramilitary force and also has its own extrajudicial detention facilities. Also attached to the Ministry of Interior is the Criminal Investigative Department (CID) of the police, which conducts most criminal investigations and arrests. The total strength of the CID is estimated to be 13,000 personnel. According to the U.S. Department of State, members of the PSO and Ministry of Interior police forces have committed serious human rights violations, including physical abuse and lengthy detentions without formal charges. In 2002 the government established the National Security Bureau, which reports directly to the president and appears to have similar responsibilities to those of the PSO, but it remains unclear how the two organizations coordinate their responsibilities.

Internal Threat: Analysts see the greatest challenge to the political dominance of the General People's Congress as stemming from a range of security threats posed by Islamist and tribal elements within Yemen. Yemen's topography contributes to a lack of central government control in the more remote governorates, which in turn has enhanced the authority of the country's well-armed autonomous tribes. Tribesmen routinely kidnap foreign tourists and workers in order to extract political and economic concessions from the government; as recently as May 2008, two Japanese tourists were kidnapped in Marib.

In northern Yemen, since 2005 al-Houthi rebels have carried out attacks against police and soldiers near Sadah; the attackers are believed to be followers of a militant Zaydi cleric killed by Yemeni security forces in September 2004. Despite the negotiation of cease-fires in March 2006, June 2007, and February 2008, thousands have been killed, and fighting continues. Several bombings were reported in May 2008. Since May 2007, in Aden and other southern governorate cities, security forces have battled demonstrations by former army officers, demanding reinstatement and better pensions, as well as unemployed workers. In 2008 these protests have grown in number and intensity. The government also faces a threat from militants from Saudi Arabia, Afghanistan, and Iraq who routinely cross the Yemen–Saudi Arabia border, as well as militant Islamists from Somalia who can access existing arms smuggling routes between the two countries.

Terrorism: Yemen was the site of two major terrorist attacks—the suicide bombing attack against the USS *Cole* in October 2000 in the Aden harbor and the bombing of the French supertanker *Limburg* off the port of Al Mukalla two years later. In 2004 suspects linked to al Qaeda were prosecuted and convicted in Yemeni courts for the Aden attacks as well as other planned terrorist activities. In 2005 dozens of al Qaeda members were tried and convicted in Yemen of planning and perpetrating terrorist attacks against Yemeni officials and Western targets both in Yemen and abroad, including additional suspects linked to the USS *Cole* bombing. On February 3, 2006, 23 convicted al Qaeda members, 13 of whom were tied to the USS *Cole* and *Limburg* bombings, escaped from the maximum-security prison in Sanaa; most remain at large. In September 2006, four suicide bombers were killed in a foiled attempt to bomb two Yemeni oil facilities; two of the four have been identified as being among the group of 23 escaped prisoners. As of June 2008, two al Qaeda suspects convicted in Yemen of terrorist attacks have also been indicted in U.S. courts and are wanted for trial in the United States, but Yemen has insisted that its constitution precludes extradition of Yemeni citizens.

Although al Qaeda continues to use Yemen as a base for training and operations, several incidents in the past two years demonstrate that the country itself is targeted for attack. In July 2007, a suicide bombing in Marib killed eight Spanish tourists; in January 2008, gunmen killed two Belgian tourists in Hadramout; in March 2008, a mortar attack that damaged a school was apparently aimed at the U.S. embassy; and in April 2008, bombs struck a residential complex inhabited by Westerners.

According to the U.S. Department of State, Yemen's recent counterterrorism record is mixed. The government has been lax in enforcing terrorism convictions, provides lenient requirements for the completion of sentences to persons who surrender, has released all 12 returned Guantanamo detainees, and lacks a comprehensive counterterrorism law. However, Yemen's government continues to arrest and prosecute the perpetrators of terrorist attacks. There is concern that Yemen's government has a limited capacity for stemming terrorism financing and has been unable to freeze the financial assets of United Nations–designated al Qaeda supporters. There are also reports that Yemeni jihadists are in Saudi Arabia, Afghanistan, Somalia, and Lebanon and that Yemenites constitute one of the largest contingents of foreign fighters in Iraq (about 17 percent of total foreign fighters in Iraq according to some estimates).

Human Rights: According to the U.S. Department of State's annual report on human rights practices, Yemen's government has maintained a poor human rights record, continuing to commit various abuses, including the arbitrary arrest and killing of persons critical of the government, especially those affiliated with the al-Houthi rebels of Sadaa. Security forces, which are generally considered corrupt, often detain persons for prolonged periods of time without due process, subjecting them to torture and abuse. Violence and discrimination against women have been reported, as well as discrimination against persons with disabilities and against religious, racial, and ethnic minorities. The ruling party often controls the management of unions and trade union federations.

Although Yemen's constitution protects privacy, government police forces routinely search citizens' property without warrants and monitor telephone, postal, and Internet communications. Yemen's constitution provides for freedom of speech and of the press "within the limits of the law," but this protection is also violated. Police forces often threaten and harass journalists who are critical of the government in order to influence press coverage; physical attacks have also been reported. Some journalists have been placed on trial for writing articles critical of the president or reporting on issues deemed sensitive to the government, and newspapers have been temporarily shut down for the same reasons. In June 2008, the editor of a weekly newspaper was imprisoned for allegedly supporting the al-Houthi rebellion; the government's action is considered by the U.S. Department of State to be part of a "distressing trend in Yemen of intimidation and prosecution of independent journalists." Foreign publications are monitored for content and subject to censorship. Legislation was enacted in 2005 mandating that journalists reveal their information sources in certain circumstances and significantly raising start-up costs for newspapers and Web sites.